SACRED

Tears

LINDSEY WHEELER

Founder of Bottle of Tears

with MARY CARVER

HARVEST HOUSE PUBLISHERS
EUGENE, OREGON

Interior and cover design by studiogearbox.com
Cover and interior photos by Amelia J. Moore

This book contains stories in which people's names and some details of their situation have been changed.

Sacred Tears
Text © 2021 by Lindsey Wheeler and Mary Carver
Photography © 2021 by Lindsey Wheeler
Published by Harvest House Publishers
Eugene, Oregon 97408
www.harvesthousepublishers.com
ISBN 978-0-7369-8173-6 (hardcover)
ISBN 978-0-7369-8174-3 (eBook)

Library of Congress Cataloging-in-Publication Data Record
is available at https://Icon.loc.gov/2020018966.

Printed in China

20 21 22 23 24 25 26 27 28 / RDS - SG / 10 9 8 7 6 5 4 3 2 1

For Chris and Eliana, my little triangle family. It feels like we've been through it all together, but we know there's more ahead. Still, I'd pick you both all over again. Every single time. Family sticks together, right? Love y'all with my whole heart.

Contents

Foreword

BY JENNIE ALLEN

I imagine that you picked up this book because of an ache in your life, a place where you are hoping for healing and restoration. You've come to the right place. I know well the gaping holes of suffering that my friend Lindsey Wheeler has lived through and the healing and hope she has fought for. In these pages, she's going to tell you her story of living through these dark days and of the healing that God has supplied to her—healing that is also available to you.

In Ezekiel 37, God makes an absurd promise in a conversation with the prophet Ezekiel. Ezekiel is looking at piles of bones, and God asks him, "Can these bones live again?" Ezekiel responds wisely: "Lord, you're the only one who knows that." Then God brings the bones back to life.

God alone can breathe life into situations where all we can see is death. The greatest hope we have in life is that we follow a God who brings life from death. Without that promise, our worst fears come true, and we truly have no hope. But with that promise, there is ultimately nothing on this earth to fear.

That is how my friends Lindsey and Chris Wheeler live. Their lives are not easy. Their story is beautiful but also full of disappointment.

Yet they have found joy—not only for themselves but also for others, as you will read.

Usually when people share about their suffering, it is in the past. But this book is unique because Lindsey is still in the middle of her suffering. Her answers don't come with a beautiful floppy bow; they are written through tears. She is feeling the pain today, right now. She is still in the middle of it. And doesn't that make her the best comforter? Isn't that who we want beside us in the midst of our pain—those who know pain?

Lindsey and Chris laugh, perhaps more than anyone I know. In fact, when I am with them, I laugh too. They are so great at laughing at life, they're contagious about it. How can two people who have endured so much be such great laughers? And even more, how could they spread laughter everywhere they go?

I will tell you, and the answer isn't complicated. They laugh at the days to come because they aren't afraid of them. They've tasted loss and disappointment, and they've seen that even in the worst that can happen, their joy in Christ cannot be taken from them.

What has brought you to these pages? Do you need hope, do you need a confidant, do you need to cry, do you need to laugh? Do you need to believe down to your bones that Jesus is enough and that one day, he will wipe every tear?

You will find a home here with these words. Whatever you are facing, my prayer is that you leave these pages with tremendous hope, that you will be reminded of God's great love for you through the Word of God, which is strung all through these pages.

The passion of Lindsey's heart has been captured in her dream of Bottle of Tears. Over these years, I've watched her ship bottles to so many people and pray for them. It has been a stunning manifestation of her contagious love, a love that she has received from Jesus and gives to everyone who knows her or is touched by her ministry. She believes down to her bones that hope is available for every tear you shed and every difficult story you might face. Prepare to experience that hope and healing in these pages. I'm honored to call her a dear friend and honored to introduce you to her in these words.

A Letter from Lindsey

Hey, y'all. My name is Lindsey. I'm a wife and mom. I struggle every day to get out of bed because of a chronic illness, but I do it because I have a child with special needs. I've been doing this for more than ten years now, but I refuse to give up hope. I know God has made me for more than just this sickness, and I desperately want to love others, even in my brokenness.

That's where Bottle of Tears comes in. It's a vision, ministry, and business that God gave me in the midst of great pain and suffering, birthed out of many hours spent shedding my own tears. We send messages of hope and encouragement in vintage bottles—some more than 100 years old—on behalf of people who order them as gifts. Each bottle includes a reminder that God knows us so intimately and cares about us so deeply, he saves each of our tears in his own bottle.

I know I'm not the only one walking a hard road. Your situation probably looks different from mine, but your circumstances and struggles may be just as difficult. Each of our stories is unique, but here's what we have in common: We are not alone. God is walking right beside us, right in the midst of our heartbreak and hard places.

I didn't always know that though. It took me a while to get here, which is why I'm so determined to share the hope I've found with everyone I meet. I spent many years wondering what was wrong with me, looking normal on the outside but experiencing constant, debilitating pain. I knew I was sick, but doctor after doctor dismissed or misdiagnosed me until I was finally diagnosed with Lyme disease.

My story does not have a Hallmark-movie ending. I'm still sick. I haven't found a neat, red bow I can wrap around the pieces of my life that will make it all look okay. I am not writing from the perspective of having been *through* suffering. I am writing from the middle of it. And I suspect I'll be in the middle of it until heaven.

So here I am. I'm broken. I'm in pain most of the day. My precious daughter, Eliana, has adoption trauma—too many struggles to list—and joy is a precious commodity we fight for daily in our little family of three. Perhaps you can relate; perhaps you too are looking for hope in the middle of hard times. Can we sit together in this place?

Let's talk about the times we've prayed but not been healed. Together, let's face the pain of broken promises, empty cribs, insurmountable debt, crushing depression, and missed opportunities. Let's not pretend it's okay. Let's not hide our tears.

The tears we cry, whether we're happy, sad, angry, confused, or overwhelmed, are *precious*. They are so precious to God that he saves them—all of them—in the most breathtaking bottles.

Lindsey Wheeler

Dear Lord, thank you for the gift of tears—the relief they offer, the way they allow us to express what's deep in our hearts, and the fact that you find them so precious and valuable that you keep them in your bottle. Lord, let me never forget that you love me. Help me remember that you are with me every moment, brokenhearted for me, and weeping with me. Keep me mindful of your presence even when I experience the deepest of pain.

Thank you, God, for loving me.

Thank you for being here with me. Amen.

You keep track of
all my sorrows.
You have collected all
my tears in your bottle.
You have recorded each
one in your book.

PSALM 56:8 NLT

CHAPTER ONE

The Birth of a Mission and a Ministry

In early 2014, thanks to the painful grip of Lyme disease, I was unable to travel to a conference I'd been planning to attend for months. Devastated to miss a weekend listening to inspiring speakers and reconnecting with dear friends, I cried as I watched the conference online. Surely this was an indication that my life was essentially over.

Lonely, hurting, and scared, I asked God what fruit could possibly be produced from my suffering. He spoke so tenderly to me in the midst of my pain and loneliness—and he gave me a vision for a business that would minister to people in their darkest places.

Bottle of Tears is an online curated gift service that equips friends with meaningful tokens of hope they can send to those who are hurting. When you don't have the words to say, a tangible gift can show someone that they are seen and not forgotten by both their loved ones and Jesus himself. It is a great privilege to partner with people committed to sharing comfort and hope with others.

I hand package every order placed with Bottle of Tears, praying over each one. I know how valuable sweet surprises like gifts and mail can be when life feels like it's been turned upside down, and I pray my bottles will be a tangible reminder to the grieving and broken that they are not alone and that their story is not yet finished. My deep desire and prayer is that our gifts will be a glimmer of hope in someone's story, pointing them to a God who sees them and loves them and will never abandon them.

God has used gifts from Bottle of Tears to speak to hurting people in ways that continue to astound me. So many times I've opened my email to find messages of thanks and stories of boxes that arrived on doorsteps the exact day someone needed hope most desperately. If ever I forget that God is in the details, that he cares about every little part of our lives, this ministry reminds me.

Once I received two orders from two people who lived on opposite sides of the country—for the same woman. As I packed the bottles they had ordered, I thought, "How sad! She's going to get two gifts on the same day. I wish they were spread out." Later, the woman who received the gifts emailed me, and I couldn't believe her story.

She told me that the two women who sent her gifts didn't know each other. It was merely a coincidence that they both chose to support her with gifts from Bottle of Tears. But that wasn't all. She shared with me that she and her husband had been in the adoption process when she got pregnant. But in the span of five days, she lost her baby

God is going to work it all out for the good.
All the pain, frustration, heartbreak.
Somehow, and in some way, he is
going to use all of the broken pieces to
make a beautiful masterpiece.

Ashley Hertherington

and the adoption fell through. She lost two children, she said, and God knew she needed not just one bottle but two.

Incredible!

For so long I thought I needed to be healthy and my daughter needed to be "okay" before I started something that could make a difference, had a ministry, or made an impact. But God said, "I want you right where you are." He said he wants to show people hope in the middle of their pain—not after it's over. And every time I say yes, no matter how weak and small I feel, that's exactly what he does.

A person who receives a bottle from our ministry might see a bit of dirt, a chip, or a crack in it, but I see character and hard-won beauty. Just like these bottles, we can become dusty or even broken by our circumstances, but still God sees beauty and purpose.

So take heart, friend! Remember that even on your darkest days, even through your most broken seasons, God is building something beautiful in your life, and he will use you to serve others if you let him.

God, you are so creative and so gracious. Thank you for using the most imperfect vessels—both bottles and people—to do something beautiful. Thank you for shining your light through the cracks and reminding us that nothing can stop your love. And thank you for the opportunity to encourage one another, Lord.

Please help me accept any encouragement you send me, and open my eyes to ways I can share the same hope with others around me.

In Jesus's name, amen.

Therefore we do not lose heart.
Though outwardly we are wasting away, yet
inwardly we are being renewed
day by day. For our light and momentary
troubles are achieving for us an eternal glory
that far outweighs them all.
So we fix our eyes not on what is seen,
but on what is unseen,
since what is seen is temporary,
but what is unseen is eternal.

2 CORINTHIANS 4:16-18 NIV

CHAPTER TWO

You Are Not Alone

Sometimes the world doesn't see your pain.

Sometimes you grieve and suffer in silence. Long after the diagnosis, the divorce, the funeral, or the first waves of depression, you find yourself still hurting and hopeless. You wonder why nobody has noticed that you're still not healed, you're still not happy, you're still not okay.

My husband, Chris, often says, "Grief lasts longer than a casserole."

Your pain is likely different from mine. You may be grieving the loss of a parent or a marriage or a job or a dream. You may be fighting depression or anxiety, loneliness or isolation, or the overwhelming pace and inevitable wear of a too-busy life. Your days may be spent in the monotony of diaper changes and soccer practices, or you may spend every waking moment caring for aging parents or children with special needs. Perhaps your pain comes from what is missing—a relationship, a child, meaningful work, financial provision. Pain takes on different characteristics; sometimes it's numbing, and sometimes it's crushing and searing. No matter what is hurting you or how, you aren't alone.

Our family recently weathered a season of swift and constant change. Though the radical changes are now over, we are still navigating grief, fear, and uncertainty. We consider this our season in the wilderness. I tried to tell myself that this wilderness season won't last forever, but depression washed over me in waves anyway. Watching my daughter struggle has been heart-wrenching, and for a long time, I was a mess. Grieving so many things while facing a shrinking budget and growing bills left me in a storm of deep, isolating sorrow. Most days my prayers were reduced to simply uttering, "Jesus… Jesus," over and over. But that was enough.

One day, I followed Chris home from a church event we'd driven to separately. As we sat at a stop sign facing a beautiful sunset, he turned around and waved. And just like that, at least in that moment, I felt like we were going to be okay. Despite the darkness—or maybe because of it—I've seen so many rainbows and reminders of God's promises, and that's what keeps me going. When it feels like this wilderness journey we're on will never end, when the twists and turns won't stop coming, it's hard not to feel hopeless and alone.

Suffering has a way of leading to isolation, which in turn feeds our fear and anxiety and tricks us into thinking we have to keep it all to ourselves. But you're not alone. The Lord hasn't abandoned

you; he sees your pain. Even when friends stop checking in and family gets tired of listening, even when you feel like you're a burden, you're not alone in your pain. God is still with you.

God is constantly demonstrating his faithfulness to me, often through those who receive gifts from Bottle of Tears. Like Janet, who was battling Lyme disease and ordered several bottles from me. One of the bottles I sent her happened to have "McConnon and Co., Winona, Minnesota" etched on it. She later shared with me that Winona, Minnesota, was the very town where this woman's disease had been diagnosed and where she began treatment. It seems random and minute, I know. But I don't think it was; I think God knew she needed to know that he sees her, knows her story, and loves her deeply. So he showed up in the midst of her story—and in mine.

When you feel like you've been abandoned, even by the Lord, take heart. Resist the urge to buy into the lie or wallow in the guilt of doubting God. He can handle it. You're allowed your doubt. But don't forget to look around for the rainbows, for the sunsets, for the smiling faces throwing you waves at a stop sign, or for the beautiful vintage bottles. Look for the small reminders that God has not left you and that he never will. That's what I'm doing, even on the darkest days, and that's my prayer for you.

God, I feel so alone. It seems like the world is going on as if everything were fine while I'm lost and overwhelmed with grief. Everyone seems to have forgotten me, tired of my sadness or maybe just unsure how to help. But I know you promise to stay with me, no matter how long my pain lasts. I know you promise to love me through this, even if it takes a lifetime.

Thank you for your faithfulness, Lord! Thank you for seeing me and seeing my pain, even when I manage to look normal on the outside.

Thank you, Lord. Amen.

The thought of my suffering and homelessness
    is bitter beyond words.
I will never forget this awful time,
    as I grieve over my loss.
Yet I still dare to hope
    when I remember this:
 The faithful love of the LORD never ends!
    His mercies never cease.
Great is his faithfulness;
    his mercies begin afresh each morning.
I say to myself, "The LORD is my inheritance;
    therefore, I will hope in him!"
The LORD is good to those who depend on him,
    to those who search for him.
So it is good to wait quietly
    for salvation from the LORD.

LAMENTATIONS 3:19-26 NLT

CHAPTER THREE

Our Hearts May Be Broken, but We Have Hope

It just takes one phone call, one word from a doctor, one (fill in the blank) to radically change our lives. If you're facing that one thing right now, I want you to know you aren't alone. The Lord hasn't abandoned you, just as he hasn't abandoned me.

When you haven't been healed, when your heart is heavy, when the reality of walking through broken places threatens to overwhelm you, remember the times you've cried out to the Lord and found relief. Remember the prayers that have already been answered. Remember that he promises to be with you no matter what challenges life presents.

Parenting a child with severe trauma has made me acutely aware of my need for Jesus in every single moment. For Eliana, one moment can look dramatically different from the next. I never know what I'm going to get from one breath to another, so I often feel as if I'm walking on eggshells. We've tried every treatment our team of medical professionals can think of—essential oils (so many essential oils!), cognitive therapy, neurobrain training, and medications. But nothing has worked. One doctor at a prestigious hospital even called her a medical mystery. We don't know what healing will look like for her on this side of heaven, and it's been awful to watch her suffer.

When I feel overwhelmed by the weight of what's going on in our family, I try to remember the hundreds of things we have to be grateful for. I remember the people who have reached out to us with everything from a kind word to money for an unpaid bill, always at the exact moment we needed it most. I try to remember these expressions of love when I think about the long road ahead, when I feel so weary and cry enough tears to fill up half the bottles in my studio. I try to remember, but when I'm forced to face unrelenting pain, sometimes I forget.

So what do we hope in and hope for when healing or relief seems impossible? For my family, these things have sent us to our knees—and they have led us to a pure reliance on the belief that God has our daughter in his hands. What gets me out of bed and keeps me putting one foot in front of another is the gritted-teeth, hanging-by-a-thread belief that God loves us even when healing doesn't come. It's the understanding that "God is good" doesn't mean "I got what I wanted." God's promise was never to remove my suffering but rather to show up relentlessly to get me through it. Remembering every big and small way he's shown up throughout my life is the proof I need

God loves to take the broken
and weak things of the world and
make them beautiful for His glory.

Angie Smith

that he cares about every cell in our bodies, that he loves us, that he will sustain us no matter how dark our days become.

Even in our brokenness, even in our pain, even in the middle of our hardest places, we can find comfort in this truth. It's hard to trust God when our pain is unrelenting and our circumstances feel unbearable. But even then, we can choose hope. Not blindly or foolishly, but with confidence that though our hearts may be shattered and our bodies may be bruised, God is still good, he loves us, and he will walk through every step of this journey with us.

That's not to say we won't be sad. But even when everything seems unclear, even in the midst of heart-wrenching pain, you are not alone. He is with you, and he loves you. He has good plans for you; it won't always be like this. You may feel the heaviness of this dark night of the soul, but dawn is coming. Light is seeping through. Our hearts may be broken, but we have hope.

Oh God, I don't think I can handle this. It's too heavy, too horrible, too heartbreaking. Lord, please take this cup from me! I'm not sure I can bear this burden, God; I feel like the world might as well be ending. In fact, I almost wish it would, because this is too hard. I know you promise to help me, Lord, but I'm not sure I can believe it right now. I can't imagine ever feeling any better than I do right now.

But you promise to help. You promise that my pain won't last forever. So I will believe. I will trust you, and I will believe you, Lord; help my unbelief! Thank you for holding me in this hard time. Thank you for being the one I can hope in. Thank you, Lord. Amen.

Be strong and take heart,
all you who hope in the LORD.

PSALM 31:24 NIV

CHAPTER FOUR

God Is in the Details

You may be wondering, "Why send bottles?" When people are facing hardships and the heaviness of life, what makes a bottle special?

The easy answer is that I love all things vintage, especially vintage bottles. I love knowing these bottles—colorful or clear, chipped or flawless—have stories, and I can't wait for them to represent hope to others who are struggling. But I also know the value of surprises and gifts when life feels like it's been turned upside down. Mail is like gold for me, especially on days I haven't been able to get out of bed. And gifts and cards from loved ones always seem to arrive on the days I have needed hope most.

My prayer is that each gift I send will be a small token to remind the grieving and broken that they are not alone. My deepest desire for each person who receives a bottle—and you as you read these words—is to know that God sees you. He loves you. There is purpose in your pain, and God is not done with you yet. I pray that in the midst of the darkness, when everything seems unclear, this can be a glimmer of hope in your story.

As I package each gift, I pray for the person receiving it, asking God to provide hope and healing. I have no idea what each person needs or which bottle will speak to them specifically, but God knows. So as I package an order, I ask him, "Please allow this gift to arrive on their doorstep at the exact moment they need it."

It's a simple prayer, but time and time again, God has answered in ways both small and dramatic.

One time a customer ordered a vintage amber bottle. So I looked at my collection and selected a very old Frank's Safe Kidney and Liver Cure bottle. It was gorgeous, and I was excited to pray over it and send it on its way.

The woman who received it emailed me not long afterward and said, "You had no idea, but my sister who died in a car accident donated two organs—her kidney and her liver." Two organs—the exact ones inscribed on this bottle I sent her. I had no idea, but God had a brilliant idea. He is so concerned with the details, so present in them. He knew exactly what that girl needed in that exact moment.

Asking God to bless a bottle might seem like a silly request. It might seem like something he wouldn't have time for, like something I shouldn't bother him with. But God has made it clear—both in his Word and in the stories I hear from those giving and receiving bottles—that he cares about the smallest details of our lives.

God knows us better than we know
ourselves, and He knows exactly what we
need and when we need it.

A.W. Tozer

Sometimes I wonder if God gets tired of my requests. I look around and see so many people in pain, enduring horrible situations that make my own circumstances pale in comparison. I think about how much worse I could have it and feel foolish for asking for help over and over. I wonder if God could possibly care or have time to mess with my little life. But God promises that every detail of my life matters to him—and every little detail of your life does too!

Every time I question, every time I doubt, the Lord reminds me what is true by showing up in the smallest, most precious ways. I hear the same kinds of stories from the women and men who receive my bottles. I see the same kinds of stories being lived out in my friends' and family's lives. I read it in Scripture and am reminded that God is in the details. He cares about every little piece of my life and yours, and not one part goes unnoticed. He loves us more than the sparrow—so much more! And he is here, offering us hope in the bottles and the birds and every big and small part of our lives.

Dear God, will you help me? These things I'm facing might seem small to someone else, but they feel so big to me. I wish I could handle them on my own, but no matter how hard I try, I can't seem to get it together. Will you send me a sign somehow? Something that shows me I'm not alone, something that proves I haven't been forgotten?

I know what your Word says, but it doesn't feel real right now. Right now I feel overwhelmed and unprepared and incapable of dealing with everything life has thrown at me. Will you help? I think you will. I know you will.

Thank you, Lord, for loving me and caring about the smallest details of my life. Thank you for taking time to show up for me, to show how much you love me. Thank you for not being small at all and for being a God of the details.

I love you. Amen.

Aren't two sparrows sold for a penny? Yet not one of them falls to the ground without your Father's consent. But even the hairs of your head have all been counted. So don't be afraid; you are worth more than many sparrows.

MATTHEW 10:29-31

CHAPTER FIVE

When Your Hurt Is Hidden

"But you look great…"

I can't tell you how many times I've heard those words over the past couple of years. The people saying them meant well, but those few words can make me feel even more alone and isolated. They make me feel completely unseen.

Whether you are battling a chronic disease, depression, anxiety, grief, or another kind of pain, know you aren't alone. You are seen, even if the source of your pain is not. As someone battling an invisible disease, I'm familiar with the pain of looking normal on the outside while suffering on the inside. I'm learning to be as honest as possible with my friends and family, sharing the full picture of my life, even when it's hard.

A couple of years ago, I sent friends and family a sweet Christmas card. The picture showed our smiling family, and the word "joyful" was front and center. We were happy when that photo was snapped, and we continue to have hope in the Lord, but we have to fight for joy. As I watch Eliana suffer every day, my journey of motherhood is filled with grief. My illness is invisible, but it keeps me in bed for days at a time. You wouldn't know any of that by looking at our Christmas card. It wasn't dishonest—we really did manage to capture a good day on camera—but it was only a piece of the full picture.

Seeking healing and comfort for Eliana has felt like putting together a crazy jigsaw puzzle without a picture on the box to guide us. Families with children with trauma rarely talk about it, so it's hard to find someone who truly understands, someone who has survived something similar. But parents like us aren't the only ones feeling isolated.

Many of us experience pain and suffering that we don't feel free to talk about. Whether you're living with a child's complicated illness or your own, a contentious divorce, devastating debt, any kind of abuse, or another situation you believe you're not allowed to talk about, I pray you find someone to confide in and the courage to share your pain with them. I pray you find someone to shoulder this burden with you, to offer you a listening ear, to stop the isolation that breeds in the dark and quiet and loneliness.

My daughter's story is hers to share, but I share what little I can because I know there are other families that are going through this. I know they're desperately searching for someone who understands, and I want them to know they're not alone. I want you to know you're not alone.

Even if we may not always understand why
God allows certain things to happen to us,
we can know He is able to bring good out of evil,
and triumph out of suffering.

Billy Graham

Do you struggle to share your full picture? If you're like me, you don't want to be a complainer or a complete downer, but you also don't want to mislead anyone by sharing only the little joys that come amid the pain. Holding the tension between honesty and oversharing is difficult, and over time it's tempting to give up and quit trying to connect with others.

But don't give up! Living in isolation can steal your joy and your hope, adding even more pain to your difficult situation. Keep searching for community; keep asking God to provide friends—the kind of friends who stick close even when the hard times last longer than anyone expected. Accept help when you need it. Allow others into your hard places for it gives them permission to let you into theirs too. Look for evidence that you are not alone and count those gifts with gratitude.

For too long I tried to face my pain alone, so I understand what it is like to be isolated. But because I've been there, I also know how vital it is to find connection, how crucial community is to our ability to withstand pain and endure suffering.

During one of my darkest seasons, my friend Jenn drove all the way across the country to visit me. She had left me several messages, and when I didn't respond, she knew things were really bad. So Jenn and her husband got in their car and drove to Nashville.

Chris and I sat across the table from our dear friends, and I told them I had simply lost hope. I described the heavy pain we were feeling and how impossible it all felt. I told them that my faith was just barely hanging on.

Gifted with discernment, my friend said, "We know you don't have hope right now, so let us hope for you."

She could have said, "Don't lose hope! You can do this! Jesus loves you," and she would have been right. But that wasn't what we needed in that moment. Instead she gave us permission to let go and offered to shoulder the burden of hoping for better days for us.

That is what inspires my ministry—the determination to simply show up for our people when they're hurting. I am privileged to provide a way people can demonstrate their love for their friends and family even if they can't cross hundreds of miles to be with them physically. I know how life-giving it can be to receive a visit or a note or a package in the mail and realize you're not alone after all.

I realize that sometimes you really have no community at all. In some seasons, friends and loved ones are truly nowhere to be found. During these brutal seasons, my desperation drives me to my knees. And often, this is when I find Jesus and am reminded that I am neither forgotten nor forsaken. Neither are you. God sees your full picture, he knows your whole story, and he will never walk away or leave you alone.

He is the friend who sticks closer than a brother; he weeps when you weep and rejoices when you rejoice. You never have to worry that you're oversharing or being too negative with him; he already knows the truth, and he has an amazing future planned for you.

God, I'm so grateful that you know me so well. Even when others misunderstand me or don't truly see me, I know you do. Thank you. Thank you for creating each part of me and for staying near me through every twist and turn of this life.

Lord, will you send me a friend who can truly see me as well? Will you lead me to someone who will understand my pain and care about my suffering? Give me a shoulder to lean on and someone who might even need me too. Help me find a community that values and cares for me.

And I will lean on you, Lord. I will trust you when you say you are close to the brokenhearted, rescuing and healing us in the most perfect timing because you love us.

I love you too, Lord. Amen.

The LORD is close
to the brokenhearted;
he rescues those
whose spirits are crushed.

PSALM 34:18 NLT

CHAPTER SIX

The Universal Language of Pain

My family's struggles are probably different from yours, but I don't doubt for a minute that you have your own story of pain and suffering.

No matter what kind of pain a person is suffering, parts of that pain are universal. Whether it's emotional pain from loss or disappointment, or physical pain from illness or injury, everyone in pain has something in common with others. One of the unexpected gifts of facing great pain in my own life has been learning to recognize my fellow travelers in this journey of suffering and sharing comfort in the sheer knowledge that we don't suffer alone.

No one is immune to pain in this life. No one truly has it all together. And barely anything is exactly what it appears to be on the surface. After all, you can't judge a book by its cover or a family by an Instagram feed, right?

Yet when we look around, we can be tempted to believe that everyone else is better off than we are. We can believe they aren't struggling, they aren't grieving or failing or wondering when things will change. And even if we acknowledge that others have problems, we may assume they can't possibly know how we feel because everyone's situation is unique.

But does it really matter if our problems are exactly the same? Or is it possible we all speak a universal language of pain?

These false perceptions—that everyone else is living an easier life or that they couldn't possibly understand our challenges—feed our sense of isolation. In fact, they are downright dangerous. They cause us to shut people out and eliminate the possibility that someone could relate to us, or us to them. These are some of the enemy's worst lies. He's desperate to make you believe that you're the only one facing this, that nobody else understands, that you're on your own. When we are isolated and cut off from the truth, he can do his greatest work, leaving an unthinkable path of destruction.

But it doesn't have to be that way.

I have suffered in isolation, but I also know the relief of inviting someone into my pain and allowing them to carry a small portion of my burden. I will never stop beating the drum for community even though I know it is so hard to find.

True community is messy after all. Even under the best circumstances, pursuing community requires a level of inconvenience and

Two are better than one, because they have a good reward for their toil. For if they fall, one will lift up his fellow. But woe to him who is alone when he falls and has not another to lift him up! Again, if two lie together, they keep warm, but how can one keep warm alone? And though a man might prevail against one who is alone, two will withstand him—a threefold cord is not quickly broken.

ECCLESIASTES 4:9-12 ESV

exertion—a choice that feels counterintuitive when you're hurting. When we're hurting, the last thing we feel like doing is reaching out. Instead, we wish someone else would see us and reach in. And that just perpetuates the cycle! It's why so many of us stay stuck in our hurt even when we're right next door to other hurting people.

We need one another. This is how God designed us. As my pastor often says, "We are the solution to each other's problems."

Knowing that so many of us are hurting in our own ways makes connection both easier and harder.

Relationships are rarely tidy. You can be efficient with your calendar, errands, laundry, and lawn work, but you cannot be efficient with people. People take time. You simply can't fast-forward the relational process. Trust is built through consistency over time.

There is, however, one exception to this rule, one shortcut to relational intimacy: pain.

Walking through pain with someone accelerates human bonding. Tragedy unites. When we hurt, we're vulnerable, and this vulnerability means we are no longer in complete control. Our weakness is exposed. This is why combat bonds soldiers to one another for life. When you've been in the trenches with someone, your stories are forever fused.

So when I'm hurting and I open up to someone else who's hurting, we form a bond quicker and deeper than if we'd been perfectly healthy and strong or if we'd kept silent about our struggles. When

I'm brave enough to tell my own story and help carry another person's burden, I find my own pain hurting a bit less.

Even if our stories are vastly different.

Sometimes it's not appropriate or even necessary to share every detail of your story. Sometimes it truly would be an "overshare." When friends get that and just trust that what I'm going through is excruciating, it's a massive gift. It's refreshing to not have to prove to someone that what you're going through is tough. In those moments when someone simply validates my pain by saying "I believe you," it far outweighs any platitudes or promises they might have shared. This then compels me to find ways to be that kind of friend for others.

In a way, that's what I want to offer you today.

Are you hurting? *I believe you.*

Is your situation difficult? *I believe you.*

Does it feel unbearable and unending? *I believe you.*

If you've been enduring a painful season, I suspect you've faced your share of skeptics, cynics, or unsympathetic individuals. I'm so sorry, friend. I know how much that hurts. If someone is courageous enough to share a portion of their hurt with you, respond to each brave confession by saying "I see you" and "I believe you." It's what we all long to hear, and I believe it's what we're called to say.

Dear God, forgive me for judging a book by its cover. Forgive me for assuming others aren't going through anything hard, for believing that my pain is so unique that nobody else could understand, for withholding compassion even though I know how much it means.

Please help me hear and speak the universal language of pain. Show me the people in my life who are hurting, and help me be a better friend. At the same time, God, please, please send me a friend who believes me and speaks my language. Thank you for being a Friend who believes me and walks with me even when nobody else has.

I love you, Lord. Amen.

Bear one another's burdens,
and so fulfill the law of Christ.

GALATIANS 6:2 ESV

CHAPTER SEVEN

Dealing with Disappointment When Your Reality Keeps Changing

Last year was a season of emotional whiplash.

Chris and I were certain that God was leading our family to move across the country, and we made several permanent steps in that direction. But then we had to face a hard truth. We weren't going anywhere after all.

We were so baffled. We had been so sure this was God's will. The decision had been confirmed through Scripture, songs, circumstances, multiple advisors, and even a dream! God seemed to be inviting us to take a giant leap of faith into a season of transition.

It made so much sense. It felt so right. We were so certain. And then it didn't work out.

Do you know that feeling? That feeling of following God or your instincts or what makes perfect sense on paper and in your heart—only to watch doors slam closed, to see opportunities vanish, to be jerked back into the situation you thought you surely were leaving behind? That feeling of surprise, of confusion, of disappointment, of grief?

This isn't the first time I've experienced this. Far from it! I've lost count of the number of times I've found a solution for a problem, pursued it with everything I have, and been smacked in the face with a completely different outcome.

Sometimes the whiplash is unseen and internal, making it especially difficult to manage. This is one of the hardest things about grief, pain, and suffering. It can feel so jarring and disappointing when things seem to be getting better, but then you're slammed with another wave of pain, depression, and anger.

But even when our world is spinning or we're spiraling in a storm of confusion and disappointment, God's goodness and his love for us remain constant. And yet, while I know that's true, it often doesn't feel that way.

This season has been a wild ride of faith with twists and turns we would never have imagined. By the time we realized we were not, in fact, leaving Nashville, we'd already sold our dream house. So instead of heading out on a grand adventure across the country, we moved into an apartment just up the street from what had been our home. And while we know it's just a thing, we deeply mourned the loss of that home. We were especially sad to leave behind our front porch.

Joy is not the absence of suffering.
It is the presence of God.

Robert Schuller

That porch saw a lot of life! Community happened on that porch. We celebrated birthdays and grieved deaths on that porch. We ate a lot of chips there, and we laughed so, so much. Time seemed to slow down on our front porch.

Saying goodbye to the daily aspects of community life we spent years building in our neighborhood made me so sad. It took an enormous toll on my mind and body, as well as my daughter's mind. Anxiety, depression, illness—in the wake of our season of uncertainty—all flared up and knocked us flat. Not a single thing happened the way we expected, and so much of what God was doing simply confused and angered me.

We were walking in the wilderness, weary and weighed down with so many questions, though we still held on to the belief that God was with us. Even as we spun in circles, trying to find direction or explanations or just a little peace of mind, he was with us. And just like every other time we've been forced to a sudden halt, God remained our constant.

Though the world around me changes at a breakneck speed, God never does. And that is the only thing I can hold on to. As the words of the hymn say, "When sorrows like sea billows roll, whatever my lot, thou has taught me to say, 'It is well, it is well with my soul.'"

Recently a customer shared her story of God's faithfulness through a tremendously turbulent time. Shortly after adopting her youngest son, who has a complex medical condition, her 37-year-old husband was diagnosed with pancreatic cancer. This wife and mother of three young children felt as if her world was crashing down around her. Understandably, she spent weeks crying and begging God for a miracle.

One of her best friends sent her a pair of earrings from my shop and a print with Psalm 56:8 (NLT) written on it: "You keep track of all my sorrows. You have collected all my tears in your bottle. You have recorded each one in your book." She shared that she'd never really heard that verse before, but it reminded her that her tears were not in vain and that God had never left her side. God used jewelry and a friend's love to show her that no matter what unexpected and unwelcome changes came her way, she wasn't alone and God would be faithful. Did it heal her husband? Nope. Did it heal her adopted son? No again. But that was never the promise, was it? God never promised us ease or simplicity; he promised us faithfulness and his unwavering companionship. And that's what she needed in that moment.

Have you ever looked at your life in disbelief, not even recognizing the mess it's become? Have you questioned God, asking why he let you run in a direction, make a change, or simply hope for healing when that wasn't his plan?

So many of us are living lives drastically different from the ones we dreamed of and planned for. And the balance between being realistic and remaining hopeful can be precarious. When our foundation is constantly shifting, it can even seem unattainable. How can we possibly be steadfast while also hopeful?

After disappointment or unexpected changes, in the midst of confusion or exhaustion, we must choose to lean on the Lord our God if we're going to stand back up. Recalibrating our understanding and expectations to accept the season we're in, the direction he's taking us, and the life we have now requires tremendous faith and courage. Our world changes with the winds, but I believe with all my heart that God does not. No matter how many times we're pushed in a new direction, we can remain confident in him. I know, easier said than done, right? This level of deep trust in Jesus takes practice. It's okay if you don't get it right every time. I sure don't.

Dear God, I do not know what's going on! I thought I was headed in the right direction; it made so much sense. But now? Now I'm completely unsure because nothing is working out like I expected. It's disorienting and discouraging. I don't know what to do next or how to even process everything.

Will you help me, God? Will you hold me steady, calm my frantic heart, give me the peace you've promised? Guide me, Lord. Show me where to go and what to do next. Please be my firm foundation.

I trust you to stay the same today, tomorrow, and forever. Thank you, Lord, for being the one I can always count on. Thank you for being my constant. I love you so much. Amen.

Jesus Christ is the same yesterday
and today and forever.

HEBREWS 13:8 ESV

CHAPTER EIGHT

Asking for Help Is a Gift, Not a Burden

I am more convinced than ever that we need each other. Before I got sick, before our lives officially spun out of control, I didn't fully appreciate that. But now I know. I know that we are better together, that we belong to each other.

Nobody likes admitting weakness, and nobody likes asking for help. It can feel embarrassing or imposing, but when you get desperate enough to ask, you'll discover something stunning—there are people out there who actually love helping. I know from firsthand experience how rewarding it can be to let people into our brokenness and to accept the help they offer. The crazy thing is, allowing others to help us blesses them too, because even though nobody likes to ask for help, most of us love to give it. Think about that. If someone genuinely asked you for help, you'd probably be honored to come to their rescue. Why, then, do we assume others wouldn't feel that way toward us?

When I started Bottle of Tears, my goal was to help people show up for their friends who feel lost or forgotten, to give people a tangible way to support their friends and family who are grieving and suffering. But somehow, I didn't realize I needed the same thing in my own life. I didn't know how crucial community would be to my survival, my sanity, my very soul.

Years ago, when I had not yet been diagnosed with Lyme disease, I felt so alone. I didn't feel like I could burden anyone by asking for help when I couldn't even say exactly why I needed it. I also couldn't fathom why anyone would want to help. Some days I still can't.

But after a season of deep loneliness, God blessed my family with an incredible community that kept me afloat when I was drowning in sorrow. Throughout each chapter of our lives, God has given us friends who are like family, friends who have sacrificed to support us, friends who have laughed with us and cried with us, prayed for us, and simply showed up when we started believing the lie that we were on our own. God has made his love undeniable by providing for us in concrete ways through people.

Our family's financial life is frequently bleak. Endless medical bills, the costs of running a small business, and a husband who works in ministry make it hard to get caught up at times, much less ever get ahead! But God has shown up in the most unexpected ways, using our community's generosity to shout, "I've got you!" More than once,

There is a sacredness in tears. They are not the mark of weakness, but of power. They speak more eloquently than ten thousand tongues. They are the messengers of overwhelming grief, of deep contrition, and of unspeakable love.

Washington Irving

we've seen the exact amount of money we needed materialize at just the right moment, helping us with medical treatments, counseling, tuition for my daughter's school, and so much more. Friends and family and even people we haven't met have made these things possible.

None of that would have been possible if I'd continued trying to do it all on my own. If I'd kept our struggles a secret—out of embarrassment or pride or a belief that nobody would want to help—I'd have missed out on the blessing of receiving, of being part of a body in which all the parts care for each other. Whenever I've admitted that I feel hopeless and helpless in the face of needs that exceed our income, God has shown up in the form of community. He's reminded me that he is with me every step of the way, that he knows my needs even before I do. And because we've had to rely on him to meet our needs, he's done all this in a way we wouldn't have understood if we'd had the money in our bank account. Thinking of the ways God has provided in the past sustains me through many of the really dark days. It reminds me how close he is even when I don't feel him.

The blessings I've received through friendship and community aren't limited to financial assistance. When I finally found the courage to build community, to meet neighbors, to vulnerably reach out to friends, I was overwhelmed by the response. So many have wrapped my family in their arms, holding us up when we couldn't stand any longer. They have brought us fajitas when I was going through a rough patch of chronic pain. They've surprised us with a free getaway in a season of setbacks and struggles. They've shown up in ways I never would have imagined possible. They've simply sat with us through the hardest days, and they've been there on the good days to laugh and tease and swap stories for hours on end. They have been God's hands and feet to us, and astonishingly, they've been grateful to us!

When friends helped us move out of our home, spending several weekends in a row packing boxes, painting walls, and hauling furniture, they called it fun and said they looked forward to it all week. What on earth?

But that's the upside-down truth of God's family. When he places us in community—and we're brave enough to be honest about our reality and our needs—he blesses us abundantly by allowing us to serve and be served. It turns out that asking our friends for help is not handing them a burden but offering them a gift.

Are you reading this in disbelief, certain you'll never have such a caring community? Are you convinced that loneliness is your lot, that nobody could possibly understand your pain? Oh friend, I understand that. I've felt it so deeply, knowing without a doubt that my

Just as our bodies have many parts
and each part has a special function,
so it is with Christ's body.
We are many parts of one body,
and we all belong to each other.

ROMANS 12:4-5 NLT

sorrow and suffering would be too much for anyone else to bear, that my pain and my many needs were way more than anyone else would ever volunteer to carry.

I've felt that crushing isolation, and I wouldn't wish that on anyone. My prayer for you today is that my story will encourage you to reach out one more time, to share your story again, to open your heart to the people God has placed in your life in this season. I pray he will give you friends who see helping one another as a gift, not a burden. I pray he will show you just how much he loves you by providing for your every need through a community that cares deeply for you. I pray he will show you ways to love your people as well as accept their love in action.

Dear God, I feel so alone. I know you say you'll never leave me, but I'm afraid maybe you have. I'm afraid you've abandoned me just like everybody else. I feel like nobody cares—and I'm afraid I'm right.

Is it possible you can send me a friend? A friend who is brave enough and cares enough to walk through this painful journey with me? I don't want to be a burden, Lord. But having a friend in this dark season would mean so much. Will you send me a friend, God? Or— dare I ask—an actual community that will share my burdens and allow me to share theirs? Will you send that to me? And help me see it and be bold enough to reach for it?

Help me, God. I don't want to do this by myself anymore. Amen.

CHAPTER NINE

Finding Purpose in Your Pain

Each of us is wired with a deep longing to understand who we are and why we exist. And for some of us, our hardship is the very vehicle to this understanding. If you feel like you're missing out on life in this season of pain or if you are afraid you no longer have anything to offer the world, don't despair. God has a plan for you, and he will even use your pain to accomplish it.

I can plan and dream and try to make good things happen, but my plans for my life almost never match God's plans for me. I can look at what the world says is important and valuable, but when I allow my soul to be quiet and listen to the Lord, I remember that his ways are nothing like ours.

Last year my company reached a milestone. Bottle of Tears filled 10,000 orders in just five years. I could hardly believe it! What God has done through this little ministry is truly incredible. I'm grateful for the opportunity to serve him and others through Bottle of Tears and also for the way he's changed my heart so drastically over the past five years.

"My thoughts are nothing like your thoughts,"
says the Lord. "And my ways are far
beyond anything you could imagine."

ISAIAH 55:8 NLT

When I began Bottle of Tears, I was bedridden. I remember yelling from my bed to Chris in another room, "I'm starting an online business!" I had been in such a dark place, ready to give up on everything, feeling disqualified from life. But I desperately wanted to live again and to love people who felt stuck like me. So when God gave me this idea for a way I could do that from home, I was reenergized. Any business-savvy person would have laughed at the idea of a woman like me starting a company, but God knew better. And he has used Bottles of Tears to bring life and hope back into my very weary soul.

I've almost quit a hundred times. I've battled feeling unqualified for the job, but I remember that this was God's idea in the first place. He assured me I can walk from my bed to my office and fulfill orders, one bottle and prayer at a time. He's encouraged me to follow the path he's planned for me and to forget about the paths I expected to walk, the ones I wanted to build myself, the ones I see others walking in their drastically different lives.

This life may not look anything like I expected, but that doesn't mean I'm not valuable. God still has a plan for me, and he doesn't require me to be healthy or strong for it to work. No, his plan was to give me purpose right in the middle of this dark, draining season of my life—and that's how I know that you too can do whatever God is calling you to do. It may not make sense, but he will help you accomplish it. I wasn't disqualified from life and love and service, and you aren't either.

I can so easily forget what God is able to do with the smallest offering. He's the One who fed thousands with a few loaves and fish, so of course he can use my broken body and grieving heart to serve his children! I often feel discouraged when I hear other small business owners talk about goals and growth and hustle. Some days, when my goal is simply to get out of bed and walk to my office, I can begin believing the lies that I'm not good enough, that I'm not capable of this thing God has placed on my heart.

Thankfully, he won't let me off the hook. God reminds me that he chose someone who was suffering to empathize with others in pain. He reminds me that he asks me simply to be obedient in what he's called me to do. I don't have to hustle to be loved—and I'm here to remind you that you don't either.

We don't need a multimillion-dollar business to make a difference in people's lives. We don't need a huge stage or a bestseller or perfect photos in our Instagram feed. We simply need to love the brokenhearted. We just need to share what we have with whomever God places in our lives. And with that small offering, he will make us a beacon of hope, reminding those around us that true hope only comes through Jesus.

When I compare my life and my family and my business to others', I always fall short. But when I allow Jesus to determine my steps and guide me, I'm never disappointed (Proverbs 16:9). He always does immeasurably more than I could ask or imagine (Ephesians 3:20).

And he will do the same for you.

Yes, friend, the Lord has a purpose for you. You may not see healing on this earth, but you will see fruit. Your purpose will look different from mine, but it will absolutely bless you and other people because God created us first for himself and then for each other.

You don't have to produce or perform to be loved. You don't have to hustle to be worthy. You just have to be obedient in what God has called *you* to do in this life. Ask the Lord to make his plans for you clear, or at least the next step, and allow him to use your pain in ways you might never have imagined. Don't believe the lies that you are not enough, that you are not capable. The truth is that nobody is, but with Christ, we all are. With Jesus we find strength and hope and purpose, even in the pain. And when we do, he can use every tear we've shed to accomplish his plans for our good and his glory.

God, thank you. Thank you for not giving up on me, for loving me so much that you have made plans for me even as my life has taken so many unexpected turns! I'm so grateful you don't ask me to be like everyone else, that you don't expect productivity and perfection before loving me and using what I have to offer.

Forgive me for trying to do it all on my own. I know now that I was never meant to do that. Help me stay focused on you and the path you've cleared just for me, Lord. Help me find the ways you're giving me to serve you and serve others.

I love you, Lord. Amen.

Being confident of this, that he who began a good work in you will carry it on to completion.

PHILIPPIANS 1:6 NIV

CHAPTER TEN

God Knows What We Need Before We Do

Never in a million years would I have thought a dog would be the answer to so many prayers. But Wilson the goldendoodle, Eliana's service dog, has made a stunning difference in our family.

In 2008, Chris and I traveled to Guatemala, where we met and fell in love with our daughter. Her expressive eyes and sweet heart (as well as hints of sass) shone through her difficult surroundings, immediately drawing us in and melting our hearts. After living with her in Guatemala for four months, we finally brought our little girl home. But our journey didn't end there. And our adoption story has not had a fairy-tale ending. It's been a brutal road.

Our sweet girl still feels the devastating effects of her traumatic first few months. Though she is the love and the light of our lives, making our family complete in a way we never could have predicted or designed, Eliana's heart and brain have suffered.

As a result, we've often felt exhausted, overwhelmed, and isolated. Doctors, prayer, therapy—you name a treatment, and we've probably tried it. But until recently, we hadn't considered a service animal. The book of James tells us that sometimes we do not have because we do not ask, and we never thought to pray for this. It just didn't occur to us, largely because I'm allergic to most dogs. But God knows what we need well before we do. He knows what we actually need when we're convinced we need something else entirely. We remained faithful in prayer for other things that might help our daughter, but God was at work elsewhere.

Last summer we learned about an organization that trains dogs in Tennessee. They had one goldendoodle available (a breed that doesn't irritate my allergies). But there was a problem. Service dogs are pricey. Chris and I have often joked that we put "all our eggs in every basket" when it comes to finding help for Eliana, but we truly didn't know how we could afford this potential miracle pup.

One of these days, I'll learn to stop doubting and worrying. When word got out that we might have found a way to ease our family's struggles—with a dog—friends and family members rallied around us to support us. It was incredible! And overwhelming. And an amazing reminder that God will provide exactly what we need, when we need it. We often joke that each of Wilson's paws, legs, or ears belongs to one of our neighbors, thanks to their investment in him.

There are miracles on the
other side of rivers of tears.

Lisa Harper

Wilson has now been a member of our family for a little over a year. We are stunned by the difference he's made, but we also sort of feel like he's always been with us. I suppose that's how "family" is. He's playful and attentive but also laidback and steady in a way that makes Eliana feel safe. His constant companionship keeps her from feeling alone and lowers her anxiety immensely. She's calmer and happier and sleeping in her own room for the first time in 11 years.

We had no idea what to expect from a service dog. We prayed that he would bring peace to our family and allow our girl to grow more independent, and he has. He's also exceeded every hope we had. More accurately, God has exceeded our hopes and expectations! God can and will use whatever means necessary to reach us and help us and show us just how much he loves us. And often it's with something we didn't even know we needed.

I have never been a dog person. But Wilson hasn't just been a gift for Eliana; he helps me when I'm struggling too. My chronic disease keeps me at home and in bed a lot, and Wilson makes sure to snuggle with me there—especially on the hardest, darkest days. God is using him to change our daughter and to bring comfort and hope to me too.

If you've been in pain for a long time, you might be tempted to give in to the frustration and bitterness of unanswered prayers. I've been there; I know how hard it is to stay hopeful when every single thing you've tried has failed to deliver any relief. Don't give up! Don't forget that God's ways are not our ways, and he has a much bigger, better perspective on the world and on our lives. He knows what's coming. He knows what we need. And he knows exactly how he's going to make it happen.

Your answer may not be a service dog, but it may not be what you expect either. It may be something wildly more than you can ask or imagine!

"I have really bad anxiety, so my helper, Wilson,
is helping me with my anger and controlling it.
This dog has changed my life forever."

—Eliana

Dear Lord, I'm so sorry for doubting you. I'm sorry I gave in to bitterness and resentment when you didn't answer my prayers the way I wanted. Please help me be more like Jesus when he prayed in the garden. He asked you to take away his burden but also made it clear that his desire was for your will, not his. I want to be like that!

God, you know what I need more than I do. I believe that. Will you show me? Will you make clear to me things I can't even imagine? Will you do immeasurably more than I've ever asked to heal my pain, to ease my suffering? Please, God, I ask you to give me the answer I need.

Your will be done, Lord. Amen.

Now to him who is able to do immeasurably more than all we ask or imagine, according to his power that is at work within us, to him be glory in the church and in Christ Jesus throughout all generations, for ever and ever! Amen.

EPHESIANS 3:20-21 NIV

CHAPTER ELEVEN

From Long-Suffering and Loss to Love and Life

Chris says I'm tough. My friends have said I'm brave. What they don't see is me covered up in bed, crying out, "How long, Lord? How long?"

Perseverance is something I never asked for but have developed over the years. My physical illness and Eliana's complex developmental trauma make life like a never-ending marathon. And our brains just aren't naturally wired to comprehend or handle that. When the finish line is in sight, when the end stays in one spot, endurance feels doable. We can accept a fixed amount of suffering. But when that pain is ongoing with no relief in the foreseeable future? It's as brutal on our hearts and minds as it is on our bodies.

One of my favorite psalms begins with the question "How long, Lord?" The author goes on to ask the Lord, "Will you forget me forever? How long will you hide your face from me?" Oh, how those words resonate with my soul! I've lost count of the times this sup-posedly tough and brave woman has despaired, begging God for an-swers, for relief, for some sign that this won't last forever.

In the darkest hours of this painful season of night, time seems to stand still. The wait is cruel and excruciating, and yet even then I know my heavenly Father has not abandoned me.

One of the things Chris and I have talked about so many times is the cost of faith. As he says, faith can be extremely expensive, re-quiring far more than we originally estimate. It requires opening our hands and continually letting go on a journey into the unknown.

It's tempting to think that when things work out, it's proof God is in control, but when life doesn't go according to my wishes, it means this thing I'm facing isn't God's will anymore. But having faith doesn't mean I see everything solved and tied up in a bow; instead, it means I believe that God's way is best no matter what it looks like. Faith means believing God is sovereign and never surprised by the twists and turns of life that shake me up. But holding on to that faith when the storms hit is so hard—and getting to that place is a process.

In six short verses, Psalm 13 works through the same painful path to perseverance that I am walking repeatedly. Starting with "How long?" it quickly moves into acceptance, trust, and even worship. The song ends with the author pressing forward and say-ing, "I have trusted in your faithful love; my heart will rejoice in your deliverance. I will sing to the LORD because he has treated me generously" (verses 5-6).

The glory of the Christian life is that we
have a hope that overwhelms grief.
It doesn't eradicate it.
It sweetens it. It overwhelms it.

Tim Keller

Even before the psalmist sees the resolution to his situation, he trusts the Lord to be there. He believes God will eventually, in his time, answer and solve and heal all things. As for me, it may take longer than the span of a short song to get to that place of surrender and faith, but when I lean on him, I eventually will. I pray you will as well.

Are you weary? Wondering why so many things are falling apart at once—or when God will answer your prayers and heal what hurts?

The journey of long-suffering is such a winding road. One moment when we think we can't endure another minute, it leads us to greater understanding and immense joy. The next moment, the path swerves back to painful reminders or devastating regressions that rip away the tender scar tissue protecting our wounds.

But through it all, Jesus is there.

When the hits keep coming…

When we can't predict or navigate a single thing in our lives…

When we don't understand what is happening or how we could possibly recover…

Jesus is there. He is right there with us in the trenches, in the mud, in the dark corner, in the pain. And he loves us right where we are—in the places and circumstances that have taken us by complete surprise but are no surprise to him.

Not only is he with us in the hard, broken places, but he also is guiding us out. Though it may happen slower than we ever would have asked, his plans and his timing are perfect. If you let him, God will give you unfathomable peace and abiding joy, working miracles in your life that you never could have imagined. Unwavering joy? Maybe not. We're human, so unwavering isn't really our thing. That's okay. Waves of joy will do when that is all we can muster. Hang in there and keep fighting for the gifts the Lord has promised.

He will wipe every tear from their eyes,
and there will be no more death
or sorrow or crying or pain.
All these things are gone forever.

REVELATION 21:4 NLT

Dear God, I am so weary, so tired of fighting this battle, so weary of feeling such sadness. Please heal me, Lord— if not my body or my mind, at least my heart. Give me your peace. Give me the deep, abiding joy that comes only from knowing you. Give me exactly what you know I need most in this moment.

Thank you. Thank you for sticking with me, for never giving up on me or leaving me alone, for using this pain for something lovely. I'm anxiously awaiting the day when I will feel no more sorrow or pain, but until then I'm so grateful you are with me, catching every last tear I cry and keeping them in your bottle.

I love you, Lord. Amen.

CHAPTER TWELVE

Finding Gratitude in the Darkest Places

It's not always easy to be grateful. When you're facing pain or sorrow, when you're fighting a battle seen or invisible, when you feel weak from the attacks surrounding you, giving thanks is the last thing you might want to do. But God asks it of us, and I don't think it's for his benefit. Digging deep enough to find something to be grateful for on my hardest days changes me.

Honestly though, gratitude can be tricky. Counting gifts and giving thanks out of obligation or even obedience feels insincere. Of course, most of us can identify *something* we're grateful for, even amid the suffering, but does it count if we also are silently listing all the details of what's painful and wrong in our lives?

My head knows all the right answers. We're supposed to give thanks in all circumstances (1 Thessalonians 5:18). We're supposed to count it all joy (James 1:2-3). I know a good life is more than simply having more blessings than burdens. But my heart has a harder

Let the whole earth shout triumphantly to the LORD!
Serve the LORD with gladness;
come before him with joyful songs.
Acknowledge that the LORD is God.
He made us, and we are his—
his people, the sheep of his pasture.
Enter his gates with thanksgiving
and his courts with praise.
Give thanks to him and bless his name.
For the LORD is good, and his faithful love endures
forever;
his faithfulness, through all generations.

PSALM 100

time with all this thankfulness. My heart is weary and worried and hurting and hopeless. My heart tends to let the difficult, the disappointing, the draining parts of life completely eclipse the good.

Do you struggle with gratitude? Have you ever been so completely covered in sorrow and pain that you couldn't dig out, couldn't find the light, couldn't possibly give thanks?

What do we do when this happens? How do we find our way back to hopeful gratitude?

For me, the only solution to a lack of sincere gratitude has been Jesus. I try to remember what he's done for me—during my lifetime and his—and how nothing the world throws at me can change that. And following his example has helped too. In his most famous prayer, Jesus asks God for just enough for today: "Give us this day our daily bread." He doesn't ask for a feast; he doesn't ask for the world. He simply asks for enough for today—enough to get through the next hour, the next minute, the next breath.

When I change my focus and begin looking for small blessings, just enough for this moment, suddenly I'm overwhelmed with things to give thanks for. And once I begin uncovering those morsels, that daily provision, I'm better able to count even the hard parts of life as joyful moments that lead me closer to the Lord.

During some of my darkest days, God has provided magical moments that make it so clear he is still with me. Here are just a few examples:

• Last summer, during an intense round of medical treatments, I felt overwhelmed and scared. In an effort to collect my thoughts and emotions, I escaped to a restaurant for lunch alone, where I was served and then hugged by the sweetest, most joyful waiter. I felt like God gave me a shot of comfort and courage through the smile and arms of a stranger that day.

• One day when we were in an exceptionally difficult season with Eliana, she invited us to an impromptu tea party she threw in her bedroom. That simple moment felt sacred. It felt priceless. And we recognized it for the gift it was, partly because the rest of that day and week and month had been so horrible.

• For three years Chris drove a beat-up Jeep with no air-conditioning and no heat. We spent every penny we had on Eliana's therapies and my Lyme disease treatments. Then out of the blue, we got a phone call from a car dealership: "We have a car for you." Confused, we drove to the dealership, and sure enough, they had a 2002 Honda CRV sitting right there, anonymously paid for and donated to our family. We were—and still are—blown away by this unknown person's great generosity! God used them (and a used car with heat and AC) to remind us that he cares about us.

These moments were special on their own, but taken in the context of our struggles, each one was an even bigger gift. From the everyday to the enormous, each of these instances made God's love evident and kept me from spiraling further into despair.

Every time I begin believing God has finally abandoned me to the darkness, he shows up and proves me wrong. He redirects my gaze to the daily bread he's providing, reminding me of his love once again. And when that happens—when my faith is restored again and I find that day's portion of peace—gratitude begins to change me.

Are you sinking into that dark place right now? Settling into the depths, where you can no longer see the light or goodness or anything worth saying "thank you" for?

Are you losing hope and growing bitter, believing that all the blessings of this world have been given to someone else?

Or are you realizing that your gratitude is only skin-deep and merely given out of obligation rather than actual thankfulness?

Friend, please believe me when I say that seeking God and his goodness will change you in the very best way. Believe me when I promise that looking for just a morsel of daily bread and then thanking God for it with all your heart is exactly what you need, though it feels impossible right now. Believe me when I say that God wants the best for you—and that starts with a sincerely grateful heart open to encouragement and comfort and peace that passes all understanding.

In the pain, in the suffering and sorrow and disappointment and even depression, let's dig deep for sincere thankfulness. Though we are exhausted and discouraged, let's allow God to show us the daily bread he's providing. Let's celebrate every little win, every morsel of goodness, every piece of evidence that points to God's unending love for us. Let's give gratitude one more try.

Oh Lord, you know my heart. You know how hard—how nearly impossible—it is for me to give thanks right now. What do I even have to be thankful for? Everything is falling apart. Everything is painful. Why should I pretend to be grateful when I'm not?

I know. I know you tell us to give thanks in all circumstances. And I suppose my situation is included in that, though I don't understand why...or how you could ask that of me.

But I want to trust you, God. I do. Will you open my eyes to the daily bread you're providing for me? Will you save me from the darkness and bring me back into the light? Will you help me obey, both in word and deed, your command to give thanks? Will you use my tiny mustard seed of gratitude to build a faith and peace that grows and grows?

Thank you, God. Thank you for what you're going to do. Thank you for loving me even in the darkest places, and thank you for everything you are giving me even when everything hurts.

I do love you, Lord. Amen.

To trust God in the light is nothing,
but to trust Him in the dark…
that is faith.

Charles Spurgeon

CHAPTER THIRTEEN

What "For Better or Worse" Really Looks Like

When Chris and I got married 15 years ago, we had no idea what "no matter what" would require of us. When we promised for better or for worse, in sickness and in health, we could not imagine how much time we would spend in the "worse" and "sickness" part of those vows. But we knew that we loved each other and that we loved the Lord, and we had faith that would be enough to get us through anything life threw at us.

Sure enough, it's been enough—but it has not been easy.

People ask us, "How do you look so happy when you're dealing with so much pain?" It's true; since we said, "I do," we've been hit with one hard thing after another. But when I say that Chris is God's greatest gift to me, it's an understatement. Friends and social media followers alike have asked me if he makes me laugh all the time—and he does. His favorite joke when I'm struggling with Lyme disease symptoms continues to be, "At least you don't have seasonal allergies!" It's ridiculous, but he knows it will make me laugh—and roll my eyes—every single time.

More than just cheesy jokes, though, our bond is built on shared values and shared experiences—two foundations we are determined to reinforce every day. For the first decade of our marriage, we rarely spent time with just each other. Eliana needed both of us at home every single night and even slept in our bed. We missed parties and gatherings with friends, and eventually a lot of those friendships fell away. We could count on one hand the number of dates we'd had.

With both of us serving as round-the-clock caregivers (and Chris often doing double duty when my own pain took over), we became weary and, despite our best efforts, disconnected. But last year we had a brilliant idea. Granted, this idea only feels brilliant to us because we hadn't thought of it before, but it has made a world of difference in our relationship and our lives.

Try-day Fridays are our new favorite thing. These began on Fridays because at the time, Friday was Chris's day off, so while Eliana was at school, we made a point to explore something new together. Though we've lived near Nashville for years, we haven't seen many of the sites. Now we're making up for lost time and lost connection, one date at a time. We've visited local museums, made our own candles at a little boutique, gone ice skating, and tried every dip offered with chips at a new-to-us restaurant.

Sing to the LORD, you his faithful ones,
and praise his holy name…
Weeping may stay overnight,
but there is joy in the morning.

PSALM 30:4-5

As we've laughed and cried and prayed our way around Nashville this past year, we've both recognized that it's not the activities we're most thankful for. It's not even the time together, although that is enormous. It's the fact that after all this time (and all this trauma), we still love being together and would choose each other over every person on earth.

Years ago, Chris and I decided that we wouldn't let the struggles in our lives steal our joy. We promised to laugh with each other and never give up. Those goals are as closely entwined as our hearts; laughter and the pursuit of joy are what enable us to keep going on the darkest days. It's not uncommon at all for one of us to say to the other, "Are we going to make it?" Sometimes it's simply a verbal cue for us to lighten the mood and remember what's true. Other times, it's a desperate plea for reassurance. Every time one of us asks the question, the other answers with just enough faith and confidence, "Yep—we're gonna make it!"

We joke that God has blessed us with spiritual amnesia, allowing us to wake up with joy after a tough night with our daughter or on days when I can't get out of bed. Of course it's not really amnesia, but it's certainly a blessing. When we read in the book of Lamentations that God's mercies are new every morning, we can only nod in understanding. *Yes, this is what the Lord keeps doing for us!* Together we choose faith. Together we choose to fight for joy. And we choose to do it all together.

I understand you may not have a loving, supportive spouse walking through your pain with you. I realize you may be grieving the loss of a loved one or the absence of someone to lean on when life is hardest. I pray that God will send you someone soon in that case and that, in the meantime, you receive deep comfort in knowing that in Jesus, you have a friend who sticks closer than even a brother and that God is near the brokenhearted and counting every single tear you cry.

And I pray that the Lord will reveal someone in your life right now who will stand strong with you as you face your struggles, someone who will assure you that you're going to make it, someone who will make silly faces or cheesy jokes, someone who will make time to try new things or enjoy old favorites with you, someone who will be by your side to make the "worse" of life a little bit better.

waited in a state of sullen excitement. All its defenders were
now south of the river. What would happen, the more anxious
asked themselves, if a force of enemy cavalry should sweep
down on themselves
the y
way
to stop

Dear God, thank you for sticking close to me no matter how bad the "worse" of life gets. Thank you for being near me when I'm heartbroken.

But Lord, I need something tangible right now. I need a person in my life to lean on; I need someone to be on my team, to fight with me and for me. Will you send me someone like that or show me who can be that person for me? And will you show me how to be an encouragement to him or her too? Give me the courage to ask for what I need and the perseverance to help someone else as well. Give us trust in you and trust in each other, and keep our eyes focused on the ways we can pursue joy even when things are the worst.

Thank you for providing exactly what—and who—I need, God. I love you. Amen.

In the hands of a loving God,
sorrow and suffering become the doorways
into the greatest and most indestructible joys.

David Powlison

CHAPTER FOURTEEN

Seeking Joy and Letting Humor Help

Our family verse is one that might not seem so encouraging on the surface. Proverbs 14:13 (ESV) promises, "Even in laughter the heart may ache, and the end of joy may be grief." Rather than being disappointed that this verse basically guarantees heartache and pain in this life, we're encouraged by the truth that joy and grief can coexist. We are witnesses that the hard times make the laughter so much sweeter.

People message me a lot asking how I continue to find joy while being so sick. I always say it's a lot of laughter and a community that won't give up on me. And obviously, Jesus. But joy does not come easy in our little family of three. We are fighting every single day for hope and healing for our daughter's little brain while fighting my own physical limitations. And the truth is, my journey of motherhood is filled with grief. Filled.

This is not how I envisioned being a mother. Every photo I see on social media of families participating in special activities and going on outings makes me ache. Our life is spent mainly between the walls of our house. When we leave, it's only for a single purpose, and we spend the entire time begging God that nothing will happen when we're in public. That makes joy hard.

But joy is a decision, a reliance on Jesus when everything seems chaotic. Sometimes life is so hard that choosing joy or finding a silver lining feels impossible. But when we remember the Lord who is always with us and never abandons us, we can find at least one reason to be grateful. And with his help, we can begin to seek joy in even the smallest things.

In Psalm 33, the author doesn't say their hearts were rejoicing because life was grand. He didn't praise God because he won a battle, got a new job, met the love of his life, or inherited a fortune. He rejoiced simply because he trusted God. That's all.

Are you able to rejoice simply because you trust God?

It's not easy! I know that for sure. Joy in the midst of pain? Maybe when everything is better, when I'm not sick, when life isn't so hard…

But no.

It's easy to think joy and suffering are mutually exclusive. They can't possibly exist at the same time. But then there's Proverbs 14:13: "Even in laughter a heart may be sad, and joy may end in grief."

Our hearts rejoice in him because
we trust in his holy name.

PSALM 33:21

God isn't actually demanding the impossible of us. He knows well that in this world, we will have trouble (John 16:33), but he's not giving up on the possibility of peace and joy in the midst of that. He's acknowledging a truth that seems folly but is actually great wisdom: Joy and suffering can and often do exist in the very same space at the very same time.

But how? How do we find a bit of joy when we're bombarded by bad news? How do we rejoice in the face of disease, disappointment, depression, and all the brokenness this world guarantees?

I've found that, contrary to my own beliefs, the times I feel the least like laughing are actually when I most desperately need levity. Though I can't always get relief for my physical pain, I can find relief and release for my mental anguish by letting go and laughing, even if for just a moment.

One of Chris's greatest gifts to me and our family is his joy and humor no matter the circumstance. We can go from crying to laughing in a matter of moments. Our daughter's service dog is so supportive of our entire family that he's taken to giving full-body hugs when he senses I'm down. And despite her trauma and illness, my daughter remains the most optimistic, determined diamond who shines just as bright as her favorite gold shoes.

Text messages from friends checking on me, an uneventful trip to the zoo (when previous attempts all ended in meltdowns and tears), knock-knock jokes, clean sheets, the voices Chris makes up for our daughter's stuffed animals, gluten-free pizza, a night at the carnival with greasy fries, exhilarating rides, and sweet friends—these things might seem like the smallest of joys a person can find, but they are mine. They are gifts from my loving Father, and I am counting every single one.

If you're struggling to choose joy in the midst of your challenges today, I pray you will try one more time. I pray God will open your eyes to the good gifts he's offering you, not as rewards he will give you after you survive the storms, but as sweet relief that just might keep you from being consumed with grief while the storms rage.

Though our family verse promises that joy and grief will mix and mingle through our lives on earth, our family motto is "family sticks together." And we do! We stick together, we choose joy, and we remind each other that we will never give up. We keep pressing forward when it feels like we're about to drown, because we know God is with us. We know he won't let us be overcome. He won't let us drown, and he won't let us down. We will be desperate for Jesus every step of the way, so we will take this life—with its pain and its joy—one small step at a time.

And that is exactly what I pray for you too.

Heavenly Father, you are so generous to me, giving good gifts and so many reasons to rejoice. Just your love is enough reason to rejoice; I know that! But sometimes it's hard to remember that. Sometimes it's hard to see anything good at all. It's hard to choose joy when the pain is so all-encompassing.

Will you help me? Will you keep me from pessimism, from negativity, from holding onto my sorrow and bitterness as if they were precious? Please loosen my hands from those things so they can be open to receive the gifts you are offering. Please show me how to smile, how to laugh—even just for a moment!—and how to choose joy even when life is unbearably difficult.

Thank you. Thank you for everything you are and everything you do. Thank you for loving me. Amen.

May the God of hope fill you with
all joy and peace in believing, so that
by the power of the Holy Spirit you
may abound in hope.

ROMANS 15:13 ESV

Conclusion

As we come to the end of our time together, I wish I had a clever conclusion or simple solution for all the ways life has disappointed or devastated you. But the truth is that I'm still walking through my own painful journey. I'm weary like you are, and the road ahead looks overwhelming for us too. And just like you, we have no idea what tomorrow will bring. As Chris says, we absolutely believe God will provide, but thinking about the things stacked against our little family makes us all want to run away!

But the nighttime won't last forever—for you or for me! The dawn is coming. Springtime is coming. Hope is coming. We know that; God promises it over and over in his Word. And you are not alone. God sees you, and he loves you. And he has a great purpose for all this pain and all our struggles. Our circumstances may be different, but our Jesus is the same. And as we sit in the middle of this hard time together, I am praying God gives you the hope you need for today.

God isn't finished with you, friend. Your story is not over. You are not alone. You are loved.

Lindsey Wheeler

Lindsey is the founder and curator of Bottle of Tears, an online gift retailer dedicated to sending small tokens of hope and encouragement to the hurting. The inspiration for Lindsey's company was borne out of her own experience as an adoptive parent and chronic pain sufferer.

In 2008, Lindsey and her husband, Chris, adopted their daughter, Eliana, from Guatemala, unaware of the deep emotional trauma their new child had already experienced. Shortly thereafter, Lindsey was diagnosed with Lyme Disease, a condition she still struggles with.

Despite the daily physical and emotional challenges she faces, Lindsey's heart is to maintain a positive outlook and find laughter and beauty in the pain, a desire she pours into every bottle she sells. Lindsey and her family live in Fayetteville, Arkansas.

About Bottle of Tears

Bottle of Tears (est. 2014) is a curated gift service through which friends and family can share comfort with one another by sending gifts of hope. What began as a way for Lindsey to use her love of vintage bottles to bring hope and encouragement to others dealing with physical and emotional pain has grown into a successful business with a diverse product line and a passionate online following.

Bottle of Tears was founded out of Lindsey's deep desire that every person going through difficult times knows that God sees them, he loves them, and he's not done with them yet. There is a purpose for their pain. Each bottle represents a small glimmer of hope in a recipient's story.

curated gifts of hope

YOU KEEP TRACK OF ALL MY SORROWS.
YOU HAVE COLLECTED
ALL MY TEARS IN YOUR BOTTLE.
YOU HAVE RECORDED
EACH ONE IN YOUR BOOK.

BOTTLE OF TEARS

Est. 2014

VINTAGE ORIGINAL

Psalm
56:8

hand packed by _____

U.S.A.

CREATED WITH LOVE IN TENNESSEE

WWW.BOTTLEOFTEARS.COM

Mary Carver

Mary Carver lives for good books, spicy queso, and television marathons, but she lives because of God's grace. Mary writes with humor and honesty about giving up on perfect and finding truth in unexpected places on her blog, MaryCarver.com. She also is a regular contributor to the online women's community (in)courage and the popular website MomAdvice.com.

A sought-after speaker, Mary enjoys giving talks to MOPS groups and at women's events throughout the Midwest. She also hosts a podcast about faith and pop culture, The Couch with Mary Carver, and has appeared as a guest on several other top podcasts. Mary lives in the Kansas City, Missouri, area with her husband and two children.

One day this groaning globe
will be renewed. Suffering will end.
Death will die.
All tears will dry. Till then be brave.
This then bliss.

Beth Moore